Poems

quite a journey

Written by

Cor Visser-Marchant

(c) Copyright 1999-2006, Cor Visser-Marchant.

All rights reserved.
No part of this publication may be reproduced, distributed, or transmitted in any form, without the prior written permission of the publisher. Small parts of this work may be referenced and quoted under under fair use legislation, provided it is clearly attributed to the author.

Bulk orders may be placed by contacting the author:
Tel/SMS: +61 416243242
Online: www.freedomphilosophy.life

Printed in Australia

Publisher's Cataloging-in-Publication data
Visser-Marchant, Cornelis PJ
Poems: quite a journey / Cor Visser-Marchant.
48p. 14 x 21cm.

Legal deposit with archives of National Library of Australia and State Library of Queensland. Free or discounted deposits with other libraries considered upon written request.

ISBN 978-0-6450743-3-8 (Paperback)
1. Non-fiction - Poetry - Spirituality
2. Healing - Mental Health - Depression.

Compilation, First Edition
Previously published online via www.poemhunter.com

My gratitude and dedication goes out to the Divine Source: Jehovah God; the great I AM who gives us the authority and power to overcome and endure.

Secondly to my wife Sally, who endured my rollercoaster journey in our early phase of marriage, without her I would not have been able to overcome the darkest of shadows.

Finally to my mother, who taught me what it takes to endure and take personal responsibility, that a parent can be fallible while never sacrificing the love for a child.

Foreword

This collection of poems, written between 1999 and 2006, has taken twenty years to bring together into a single publication. They were never written for this purpose, nor for broader general consumption. These poems are the result of the inner cathartic process of reflection and introspection, occurring during a multi-year period of severe clinical depression. I put this publication together for general interest and in the hope that it may help others in the same battle.

To those who may know me, I warn against any emotional attachment. While these do reflect thoughts that came up for me in a difficult period of time, they are simply that - my personal thoughts. The past is the past and there is no need to either re-live this period, nor for anyone to emotionally reflect on their projection of what my experience may have been at that time.

As soon as reading this is starting to affect you (the reader) emotionally, please pause and take some time to reflect on why that is, and what thoughts come up and why. Cast aside anything that is not positive or constructive for you personally in that moment - do not dwell on the past (it cannot be changed) - do not dwell on your possible future (it may never happen). Just remain in the moment, accept the blessings and look at all the good that surrounds you right now. I also recommend you to read the chapter on building resilience in my book *New Perspectives*. For general life principles, my book *Message in a Bottle* helps conquer any inclination to stepping into victimhood.

Ultimately I overcame this dark period in my life when I took full personal responsibility over my mental states and decided it was time I did so. With support I slowly weaned off the medication in contrast to psychiatric advice (*Against the*

Grain) - turns out at some point the ever increasing dosage with its side effects took over my symptoms and created a never-ending spiral the doctor never picked up on.

The lesson in this is to accept and take full personal ownership over your mind and mental states - you have agency and complete power over the thoughts and feelings you hold onto - IF you are willing to accept it. Mentally speaking, you are NEVER a victim: nobody can make you think or feel anything if you won't let them.

Cor

Table of Content

Another Memory	7
Native Land	9
The Blocked Tear	11
Life in a Box	12
Spiritual Reality	13
Love	14
We Live in Vain	15
A Choice Made	16
Misplaced Rendevous	17
The Box	18
Divorce	19
Love is the Answer	20
Velvet Lady	21
One of Seven Heads	22
Subtle Memory	23
Against the Grain	24
Two Lost Souls	26
Humility	27
Baby in the Dark	28
My Vision	29
The Game of Life	30
The proud feeling of being Dad	31
Lost the Fight	32
A Nice Pair of Shoes	34
An old man's shadow	35
Darkness of the Day	36
Life again is Life	37
Untold Blues	38
Pain	39

Another Memory

Another coffee,
Double sugar to wash away the taste
The bad taste of a memory stored.
Want to forget
But that is not allowed
Got to live through it over again, again

I love him so much
Hope I don't loose him too
Our parent's divorce couldn't keep us apart
Two separate ways
A life led, left, a new one born
Got to teach him the right way
The pressure's on!

Another tear
My first sip: double sugar
A baby's cry in the background
I have to do it right.

Life is far apart
But love doesn't know distance
The next world
We will meet again.

Aggression comes and goes –
Got to keep it down
Lay low

Love is my support
Reach out to the Divine
It's hard enough

A life led, left, a new one born
Got to teach him the right way
The pressure's on!

To write is to say
To say is to remember
Go through the pain
Talk it over, but no ears to listen
In a land far away
Music to muffle the sadness
Another thought comes by:
"Oooooh oooh.....I can't take anymore..."

Another coffee to wash away the taste
That's how we justify
Justify our lives
Can't change the past
Taste the memory while it lasts
Got to do it right from now

Until we meet again!

Native Land

Why can't I let it go
The native land pulls again
I've travelled the world & lived
Lived happily until I found true love
Try to live a family life
People say it will pass
"The grass is greener there"; my mind says

childhood memories, family bonds
the past was, the future pulls
Social, Space, but no social space
A dream lived, but not for real
Live for her, try my best
Make it right the first time
Try not to look back

Feel the call, people rely
My strength helps, me and others
Doing it tough

Next flight? Can I get a job?
Will I still fit in?
Everything has changed
Memories bound to the lyrics
Twenty two years, can't forget the past

Can't live someone else's future
Who do you wanna kid?

My blood's the colour of my past
Magnetised by the native land

Pulled by memories
Sucked in by a love far away
My new life
Cocktails of love and past
How does it taste,
Will it last?

Native land
Does it remember me
How would I feel
Too much at stake
Can't gamble someone else's life
Why does it happen to me?

Is it the greener grass
Or the memory?

The Blocked Tear

Memories from a time long ago
Are never far away for the active brain

Music brings out the sadness of joy
Feelings of hope, love loss

The active mind never rests
It has to move to stay sane

Love was, is and never will
Be thoroughly understood
As we struggle along a rocky path

This is what we call life

Always a tear
In the darkest corner of the eye
No one knows

The tear trying to break through
never mind
another lost, not shed

the memory stays,
relived again!

Life in a Box

Possessions, life summarised in one box
My life.
Not allowed to put them out
The treasures of two fluffy toys,
Once shared with my brother.
Separate ways
The toys stay
Everything else in one box under the bed.
Flowers of ice on the wall
Leave their marks as the box gets weaker,
But memories grow strong!
Forced to stay, but no dignity left
All was left behind
The love of one person makes strong,
As on this day each year I remember
But I remember every day, I say,
Thinking back of then,
Where she was a victim of her life.
Mine is not that bad after all
Or is it still the same?

Spiritual Reality

Purity
Something to aim for, Something to hold on to
Something to fight for, Something real
The war is on

Spiritual reality.
Can't touch, can't see, can't hear
Yet it is around us everywhere

This world, The next world
Life is real, Emotions are real
Nobody's right, Nobody's perfect

Perhaps the Source,
That drives us all

Feel the power of Divine
It flows so close,
But yet so far

How can we reach?
The road is long and the journey hard
Will we get there in the end

Spiritual Reality
Virtual Reality?

Love

Where will I go?, my mind says
Afraid of the truth,
Aiming for a high.
Too detached from my inner soul.

Scared to think
Life is good on this earthly plain,
If you can stand the pain.

All is recorded in the book of life:
One's memories don't lie
It's the intentions that matter.

Mind over matter,
This life and the next.
I want to do it right
Not for selfish reasons,
But for love.

Have to relax
Approach it from within,
Not through analysis

Get in touch with the divine
Then
She'll truly be mine
(forever)

We Live in Vain

We live in vain
On this earthly plain
Just to die all the same

Then the curtain falls
And heaven calls
There we'll meet again

Our true life starts
We continue life
As we were on this earth,
But lack of space and time
Makes that
The language of the heart will thrive

A Choice Made

(in memory of Aiso)

The gun: the source
The bullet: the end
Death is relative,
A choice we can make,
But is the curtain we expect final?

The afterlife prevails
It has all been a choice made too soon
The choices we make,
The life we lead,
The curtain falls
We are

Who we are is based on the thoughts during our final moments
Although it ends,
It doesn't stop

I hope you made the right decision
Love prevails
Until we meet again.

Misplaced Rendevous

What is expected of those that grow up?
Perception is reality, reality is perception
Man is child, child is man
Life is truth, truth is life?
Maybe we all got it wrong

It's the inner child in man that never dies
Freedom is needed, love never lies
The animal within comes out
Alcohol makes the mind give in

How strong is the love to protect
Is it innocent or just weak?

A love destroyed, a passion lived
True love defies reality
Strength comes from love
Is it there?

The Box

Saturday morning
Again sucked in by the box
The mind numbs
The entertainment flows

Day after day we sit
Paralysed
As the mind goes

Precious energy used
Resistance is futile
A life ruled by sound and vision;
When will we break free?

Pull the plug
Throw away tv
Only then there will be,
Just you and me.

Divorce

Daddy's gone
A car awaits
The stranger waves

Mum says we're running late
Running away
Escaping faith

Leave behind
All but mind
We have to go

Turn around
One last look
The car is packed
(a neighbour asks)

another marriage lost,
a new life to build
"we'll be fine"

that was many moons ago

Love is the Answer

Pollution, war, disaster
Is it the end
Can love be the answer

Love is all
Forgiving and friendly
Eternal, Divine

Good, bad, ugly
Love is with all
You have the answer

Make up your mind
If you want to be kind
God will be with you

Our problems today
As big as can be
Love can protect
Both you and me

Love is the answer
(The only road)
If we could only see
The bigger picture

Love
Our only possibility

Velvet Lady

The velvet lady came
I crashed and burned
Then revived
I still survived
And now
Start to live again

One of Seven Heads

Divine Love is ever present
Even in a mid-war dream
Where vision is blurry

Oh Lord, please hurry
The dragon's blowing steam
Mirage at first,
Focus later
(make my vision re-appear)

True life is in 3D
Although we like to be...
We really are,
Lost at sea

New Jeruzalem descends
Turns my nightmare into an end
Divine providence at work
In my one-man-band

My eyes now opened
The mirage has gone
Once more I feel at home

Thy will was done
Again

Subtle Memory

A restless thought
Trying to break out
Yet, remains underground until
We hear another familiar sound

Truth is always,
But not always clear
Clearly hidden in the past
Who is right,
Or, rightfully you?

In search for myself I found,
Well, nothing yet
Mere cliché thoughts and dreams
Shut doors, afraid to open
Emotions, powerful bursts

Soon
Soon I will find me
And shall be happy with myself

Family responsibility
Prevented me
From being me, although
Now I start to see...

Myself as ME

Against the Grain

As we hear the rain tap softly on the window
Our minds wake up and compare
Compare our life with misery

It must have been on a day like this
Were my esteem secretly caved in
Dark clouds drifted in
Into my reality
Without a clear frame and ribbon
Even without a card

The gift of depression was handed on to me, and
Slowly the ghost of the past affected the present
As the brightness of life became too tough
I got used to the shade

A new dark teint of reality set in
Unknowingly the perception of truth slid to the right
Even though I now know it was wrong
The brick wall was hit, then hit again
The alarm went off and I woke up
Just enough to take a step

Sliding scales never fail
Efexor came through the door
Like wearing pink glasses:
Life is more rosy, but fuzzy
Love gained another change

And broke free

Life's true perception no became
My ultimate reality
Six months became a week-and-a-half against the grain
I guess, with the help of my wife
I can now stand on my legs again

Interests appear
Life flows freely
Hoping the thrust was strong enough
To shift my brain back to the left

Thank you all for your support
It is through you that I maintain
And not insane
Waking up loving life again

Two Lost Souls

Two lost souls
Struggling to retain their own identity
Yet, yearning for the eternal
Enjoying the pleasures and pain of daily life.

The strangers walk past,
Not knowing the internal flame
The flame that is battling to survive

What was once common ground
Has now become the aureal aim
The string's cut, but wings stay
Love survived, Lust regained,
Forever... again?

Humility

Counselling was weak
Something purely for the meek
Counselling for those in need,
Was paying for a friend.
How pitiful indeed

Counselling, I thought
Is not for me
To think that I am strong

But, oh boy
Was I wrong
Now humility sets in
Realising my mistake
Apologising in my mind
Because I was the fake

How overwhelmingly peaceful
Being able to find someone
Someone who understands
Perhaps paying for a friend indeed
Was my greatest need.

A listening ear,
No critique
Reflecting on my past
To find out what it is I seek

The invisible brick wall is crumbling under the light
The light shining on my life.
Now I am less judgemental on my wife

Baby in the Dark

Crying little baby
Waiting in the dark
Crying little baby
Waiting for a voice

Sorry little one
We haven't got a choice
Stressful for us all
To listen to your call

Mamma needs a break now
We want you to be still
So have a little peace now
Let mommy have her will
Later we will play
Oh, won't that be a thrill!?

See your bigger brother
Sure I know you see
He too can be a bother
Trying to assist you,
But keeping you awake

Yes we have our hands full,
But Love...
You both get still

My Vision

Silence! Silence!
Listen to the drum.
Music & Sound,
A familiar voice

Let's drink some more
Let the music flow
Make your sorrows go

Echoing memories from the past
Enjoy your moments,
while they last.

The happiness of mind
Rest in a single moment
Decisions to make
Futures to save

Control the flow
A world apart
It may never be so

All depends on the invested time of life.
(I love you still)

The Game of Life

We are all pawns
In a divine game of chess
Are we really in control?
Have we been given the freedom?
Or is it structured life?

The cognition fails
If we are in control,
Were is the user's manual?

Spiritually drained
Mentally strained
A better half is all we need
in order to regain ourselves

or are we never going to meet?

The proud feeling of being Dad

Two shiny blue eyes
Staring at me intensely
Scanning for guidance
In a frame of mind
Were no past-tense exists

What their future holds
Lies heavily in my hands
Like a grain of sand
Carried by the waves of the ocean

Their brains are moved by my spirit
What a responsibility it is
To think a role model is within
..as if there is an option.

The gift of life indeed
Is equalled only by being given a child
Happy memories mixed with sad
Guide me into parenthood
Wow...

Thank you Lord

Lost the Fight

(in memory of Andrew)

All waves are gone
The machine turned off

Life is incredible that way;
A wedding on the one day,
A suicide the next.

Now part of the bloodline is lost.
Through the curtain seemed a better choice

Sadness and shock,
A speechless act.
It has drawn the family close
Hoping that the strength is there
All sympathy remains
Condolences are being past on
The good Lord was witness to it all

Today a sign said:
"Don't worry about tomorrow,
the Lord is already there!"
But the choice to end is real.
It is, for those to know
A choice to start again

To start a new life
This time without the struggle of

our modernised society
Now the pressure is off
I hope the choice was right!

For the ones left behind:
"May the emptiness at heart
be filled with solid memories!"

A Nice Pair of Shoes

To walk through life
Is to walk through shadows

To walk through life
Is to walk away fears

To walk through life
Is to walk with tears

To walk through life
Is to walk towards Love

To walk through life
Is sometimes very tough

To walk through life is .....
Well, lets walk together!

An old man's shadow

Little man
Little boy inside
A cry for help

Distance, why?
I don't want to die
Lonely heart
Driven apart

Ghost from the past
Is hunting for food
Dark memories
They last

Decided for good
No help today
Oh why is it so?
I have too much to say

Poor little man
With a sorrowful heart
I know your pain
It's made you hard

Relax some more
And live more smart
Hear God's call
And open your heart

Darkness of the Day

The darkness comes,
The darkness goes,
While the sun is still alive.

Flat memories flowing through
Why can't I feel the high?

I cry out from beneath
Hungering for joy,
But no one hears
'cause I withdraw...
to stay in bed til five.

Slowing down and easing off
It makes the brain go numb,
As in a picture slow.
My life goes by, very fast
Leaving me behind.

Ceasing life or ceasing meds
It's just a simple thought.

Life again is Life

"Life is life",
the tears cry out
Walking through the mall

I have survived
But they don't know
What it's like to fall

Light is life
Now I can see
That what I have is all

Untold Blues

(the tears begin to flow)

Remember the tears
Those trying to break through?
It seems at last
They found the door,
But I don't have the key

As they fall
Flowing to the ground
My mind feels numb and sad
Where are they coming from?
What have I found?

I need to ascertain
Head into battle
And not refrain
To try and understand
What is my pain

I may not have the key,
So is it really me?
What am I crying for
Why am I feeling sad
Is there something to be seen?
Is my life that bad

I guess perhaps its not
But then again perhaps

To tell you something new
Reality has nothing to do with it

Pain

Pain, I feel the pain
And try to ascertain
What it is
What is there to gain?

Pain, I feel the pain
The emotive rain
Rolling in
Emotions rolling in again.

Pain, I feel the pain
Ebb and flow
Tidal waves
Feelings coming in on a tidal wave

Pain, I feel the pain
And try to ascertain
What it is
What is there to gain?

Pain, I feel the pain
I cannot control
The flow
How to gain, and keep out the rain.

Pain, I feel the pain
The emotive rain
Rolling in

Emotions rolling in again, again, again.

Pain, I feel the pain
And try to ascertain
What it is
What is there to gain?

* * *

Pen dates

1999

Another Memory	21 January 1999
Native Land	5 February 1999
The Blocked Tear	8 May 1999
Life in a Box	8 May 1999
Spiritual Reality	9 May 1999
Love	19 May 1999
We Live in Vain	26 July 1999
A Choice Made	14 June 1999
Misplaced Rendevous	3 October 1999
The Box	23 October 1999
Divorce	23 October 1999
Love is the Answer	25 October 1999

2000

Velvet Lady	15 January, 2000
One of Seven Heads	15 January, 2000
Subtle Memory	20 November 2000
Against the Grain	27 November 2000
Two Lost Souls	3 December, 2000
Humility	3 December, 2000
Baby in the Dark	10 December, 2000
My Vision	13 December, 2000
The Game of Life	14 December, 2000
The proud feeling of being Dad	15 December, 2000
Lost the Fight	17 December, 2000
A Nice Pair of Shoes	24 December 2000

Pen dates

2001

    An old man's shadow   8 June 2001

2005

    Darkness of the Day   9 May, 2005
    Life again is Life   21 May, 2005
    Untold Blues   5 July 2005

2006

    Pain   3 January 2006

Other books by same author

New Perspectives
a fresh look at common spiritual topics

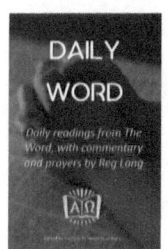

Daily Word
daily readings from The Word, with commentary and prayers by Reg Lang

Message in a Bottle
thoughts on classical liberalism and Australian politics

www.ingramcontent.com/pod-product-compliance
Lightning Source LLC
Chambersburg PA
CBHW032019290426
44109CB00013B/715